ARTIST TRANSCRIPTIONS® SAXOPHONE

THE Sonny Stitt COLLECTION

T0084126

Transcribed by Timo Shanko

Photo by William "PoPsie" Randolph
www.PoPsiePhotos.com

ISBN-13: 978-1-4234-1092-8
ISBN-10: 1-4234-1092-0

HAL•LEONARD® CORPORATION
7777 W. Bluemound Rd. P.O. Box 13819 Milwaukee, WI 53213

Contents

5 After Hours

8 Autumn in New York

10 Back Door

14 Body and Soul

18 Constellation

28 Easy to Love (You'd Be So Easy to Love)

31 I Can't Get Started with You

34 I Know That You Know

40 Moten Swing

45 On the Sunny Side of the Street

48 Orange Ashtray

53 Ray's Idea

57 Soul Shack

64 Tune Up

Biography

Sonny Stitt was born in Boston in 1924. He grew up in Saginaw, Michigan within a very musical family. His father taught music at the college level, his brother was a concert pianist, and his sister was a singer. His own musical training began at age seven, first on piano and then on clarinet.

He toured with Tiny Bradshaw in the early '40s before joining the Billy Eckstine Orchestra in 1945. Over the next several years he played on some of the early, classic bebop recording sessions, with Dizzy Gillespie, Bud Powell, and J.J. Johnson, among others.

Heavily influenced by Charlie Parker, Stitt worked exclusively on the alto saxophone on these early recordings. He often used Parker's favorite melodic formulas, and imitated his tone quality and vibrato. Stitt began to develop his own style when he took up the tenor and baritone horns in 1949, quickly becoming one of the great tenor sax players.

Stitt led a variety of groups throughout the 1950s, often assembling them as needed for each new engagement as he traveled from city to city. In the '60s and '70s, he played with a number of notable groups, including the Miles Davis Quintet and The Giants of Jazz.

He suffered a heart attack and died in 1982.

Discography

After Hours – *Sonny Side Up* (Verve 314 521 426-2)

Autumn in New York – *Compact Jazz* (Verve 314 513 632-2)

Back Door – *Goin' Down Slow* (Prestige PRCD-24276-2)

Body and Soul – *Compact Jazz* (Verve 314 513 632-2)

Constellation – *Constellation* (Muse MCD 5323)

Easy to Love (You'd Be So Easy to Love) – *Personal Appearance* (Verve MG V-8324)

I Can't Get Started with You – *Tune-Up!* (Muse MCD 5334)

I Know That You Know – *Sonny Side Up* (Verve 314 521 426-2)

Moten Swing – *Compact Jazz* (Verve 314 513 632-2)

On the Sunny Side of the Street – *Sonny Side Up* (Verve 314 521 426-2)

Orange Ashtray – *Goin' Down Slow* (Prestige PRCD-24276-2)

Ray's Idea – *Constellation* (Muse MCD 5323)

Soul Shack – *Night Letter* (Prestige PRCD-24165-2)

Tune Up – *Tune-Up!* (Muse MCD 5334)

After Hours

Words by Robert Bruce and Buddy Feyne
Music by Avery Parrish

D7
A7
Bm7
E7
A7 A7/C♯ D7 D♯dim7
A7/E F♯m7 Bm7
E7
A7
D7
A7
D7
A7
Bm7
C♯m7
F♯7
Bm7
E7
A7 A7/C♯ D7 D♯dim7
A7/E F♯m7 Bm7 E7
A7
D7
A7
D7

A7
Bm7 E7 A7 A7/C♯ D7 D♯dim7
A7/E F♯m7 Bm7 E7 A7 D7
A7
D7
A7 Bm7 C♯m7 F♯m7
Bm7 E7 A7 D7 A7 E7 A7
D7 A7 D7 A7
C♯m7 F♯7 Bm7 E7 A7 A7/C♯ D7 D♯dim7
Fade
A7/E F♯m7 Bm7 E7 A7 D7 A7

Autumn in New York

Words and Music by Vernon Duke

Dmaj7
Gmaj7
F♯m7
Em7
Dmaj7
Am7
E♭7
D7
Gm
C7
Dm
A7
Dm7
D♭m7
Cm7
F7
B♭
E♭7
B♭
B7
Em7
F♯m7
Gm7
A7
N.C.
Dm(maj7)

Back Door

By Sonny Stitt

Bm7 E7 Am7 D7 G E7 Am7 D7
G F♯m7♭5 B7 Em7 A7
Dm7 G7 C7
C♯dim7 G Am7 Bm7 E7
Am7 D7 G E7♭9 Am7 D7♭9
G F♯m7♭5 B7 Em7 A7 Dm7 G7
C9♯11 C♯dim7 G Am7 Bm7 E7
Am7 D7 G E7 Am7 D7
G F♯m7♭5 B7 Em7 A7 Dm7 G7♭9 C9♯11
C♯dim7 G Am7 Bm7 E7

Am7 D7 G E7♭9 Am7 D7♭9
G F♯m7♭5 B7 Em7 A7 Dm7 G7♭9
C9 C♯dim7 G Am7
Bm7 E7 Am7 D7 G E7♭9
Am7 D7♭9 G
Piano Solo
59
Bass Solo
23
Stitt Solo
G F♯m7 B7 Em7 E♭7
Dm7 G7♭9 C C♯dim7 G Am7
Bm7 E7 Am7
D7 G E7 Am7 D7
G F♯m7 B7 Em7 A9♯11 Dm9 G7♭9

C9♯11
G
Am7
Bm7
E7
Am7
D7
G
E7
Am7
D7
G
F♯m7♭5
B7
Em7
E♭7
Dm7
G7♭9
C9♯11
G
Am7
Bm7
E7
Am7
D7
G
E7
Am7
D7♭9
G
F♯m7
B7
Em7
A7
Dm7
G7
C9♯11
C♯dim7
G
Am7
Bm7
E7
Am7
D7
G
C7
D7
G7
G9♯11

Body and Soul

Words by Edward Heyman, Robert Sour and Frank Eyton
Music by John Green

B♭ Tenor Saxophone

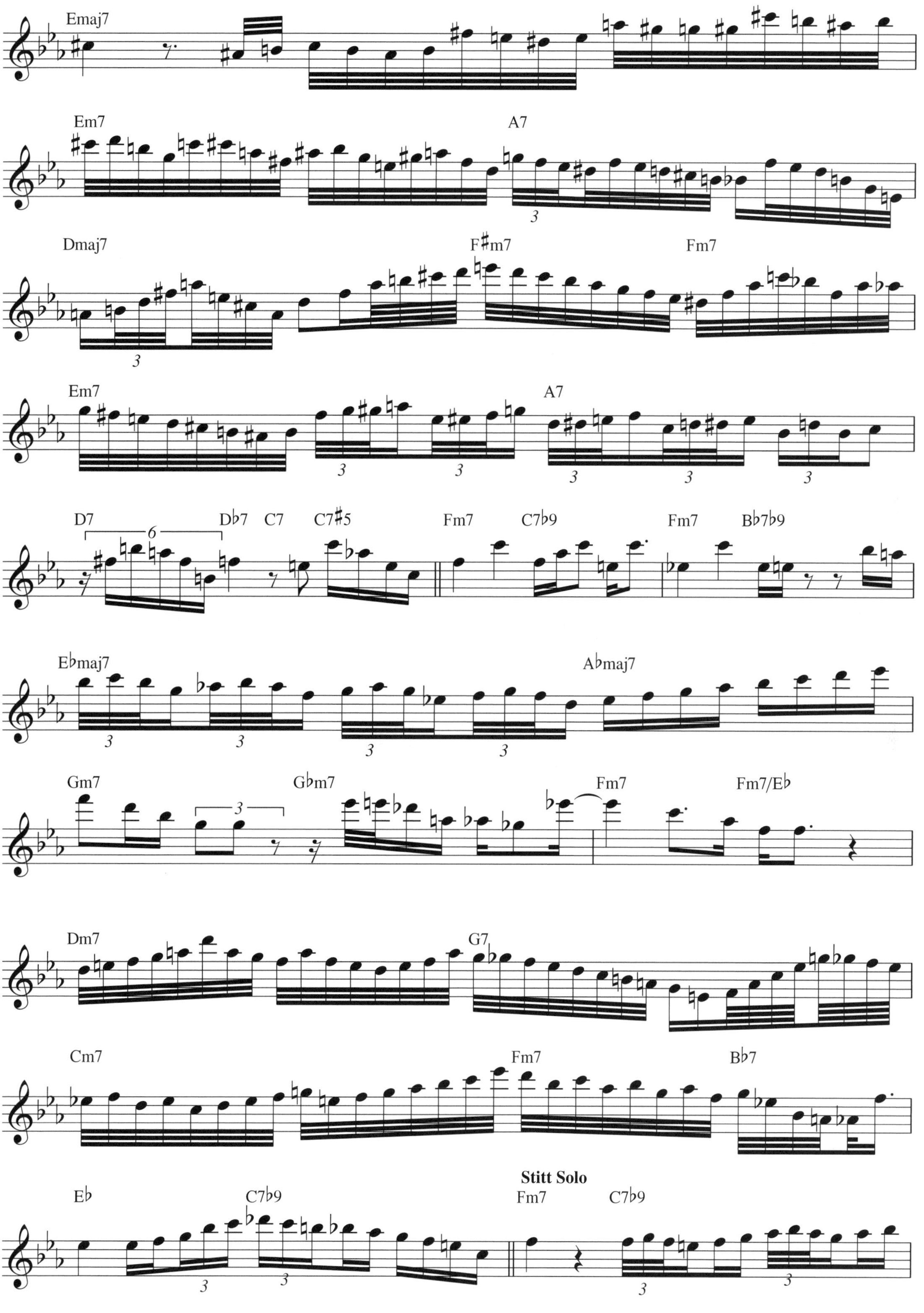
Emaj7
Em7 A7
Dmaj7 F♯m7 Fm7
Em7 A7
D7 6 D♭7 C7 C7♯5 Fm7 C7♭9 Fm7 B♭7♭9
E♭maj7 A♭maj7
Gm7 G♭m7 Fm7 Fm7/E♭
Dm7 G7
Cm7 Fm7 B♭7
Stitt Solo
E♭ C7♭9 Fm7 C7♭9

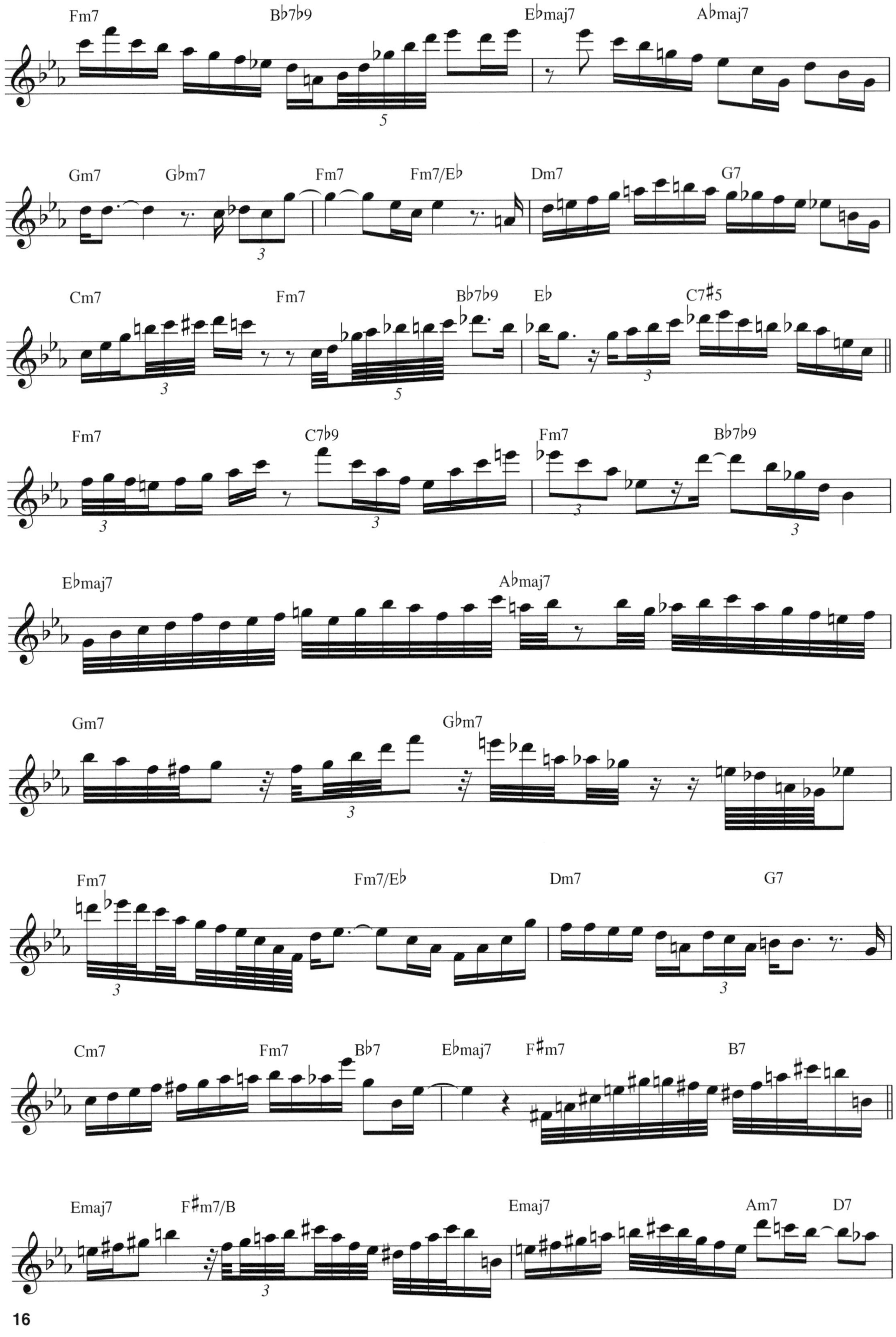
Fm7
B♭7♭9
E♭maj7
A♭maj7
5
Gm7
G♭m7
Fm7
Fm7/E♭
Dm7
G7
3
Cm7
Fm7
B♭7♭9
E♭
C7♯5
3
5
3
Fm7
C7♭9
Fm7
B♭7♭9
3
3
3
3
E♭maj7
A♭maj7
Gm7
G♭m7
3
Fm7
Fm7/E♭
Dm7
G7
3
3
Cm7
Fm7
B♭7
E♭maj7
F♯m7
B7
Emaj7
F♯m7/B
Emaj7
Am7
D7
3

G♯m7 C♯7 F♯m7 B7
Emaj7
Em7 A7
Dmaj7 Gmaj7 F♯m7 Fm7
Em7 A7
D7 D♭7 C7 C7♯5 Fm7 C7♭9 Fm7 B♭7♭9
E♭maj7 A♭maj7 Gm7 G♭dim7 Fm7 Fm7/E♭ Dm7♭5 G7♭9
Rubato
N.C.
E♭maj7

Constellation

By Charlie Parker

G7 C G Am7 D7
G E7 Am7 D7 G E7 Am7 D7
G7 C G
B7 E7
A7 D7
G E7 Am7 D7 G E7 Am7 D7
G7 C G
G E7 Am7 D7 G E7 Am7 D7
G7 C G Am7 D7

G E7 Am7 D7 G E7 Am7 D7
G7 C G
B7 E7 A7
D7 G E7
Am7 D7 G E7 Am7 D7 G7
C G G E7
Am7 D7 G E7 Am7 D7 G7
C G G E7 Am7 D7
G E7 Am7 D7 G7 C

G B7
E7 A7
D7
G E7 Am7 D7 G E7 Am7 D7
G7 C G
G E7 Am7 D7 G E7 Am7 D7
G7 C G Am7 D7
G E7 Am7 D7 G E7 Am7 D7
G7 C G

B7 E7
A7 D7
G E7 Am7 D7 G E7 Am7 D7
G7 C G G E7
Am7 D7 G E7 Am7 D7 G7
C G Am7 D7 G E7
Am7 D7 G E7 Am7 D7
G7 C G
B7 E7

A7 D7
G E7 Am7 D7 G E7 Am7 D7
G7 C G
G E7 Am7 D7 G E7 Am7 D7
G7 C G Am7 D7
G E7 Am7 D7 G E7 Am7 D7
G7 C G
B7 E7
3
A7 D7

G E7 Am7 D7 G E7 Am7 D7
G7 C G
G
Piano Solo
63
Chorus
G E7 Am7 D7
3
G E7 Am7 D7 G7 C
3
G Am7 D7 G E7 Am7 D7
G E7 Am7 D7 G7 C
3
G B7
E7 A7
3
D7 G E7 Am7 D7

G E7 Am7 D7 G7 C G
G E7 Am7 D7 G E7
Am7 D7 G7 C G
Am7 D7 G E7 Am7 D7 G E7
Am7 D7 G7 C G
B7 E7
A7 D7 G E7 Am7 D7
G E7 Am7 D7 G7 C
G G E7 Am7 D7

G E7 Am7 D7 G7 C
G Am7 D7 G E7 Am7 D7
G E7 Am7 D7 G7 C
G B7
E7 A7
D7 G E7 Am7 D7
G E7 Am7 D7 G7 C
G G E7 Am7 D7
G E7 Am7 D7 G7 C G Am7 D7

G E7 Am7 D7 G E7 Am7 D7 G7
C G B7
E7 A7
D7 G Am7 D7 G
Am7 D7 G C G
G13♯11
Cadenza
N.C.

Easy to Love

(You'd Be So Easy to Love)

Words and Music by Cole Porter

Stitt Solo

Em7
F♯m7♭5
B7♭9
Em7
A7
Dmaj7
G13♯11
F♯m7
B7
Em7
A7
Dmaj7
F♯m7♭5
B7
Em7
A7
F♯m7
B7
Fm7
B♭7
Em7
F♯m7♭5
B7♭9
Em7
A7
Dmaj7
G13♯11
F♯m7
B7
Fm7
B♭7
Em7
Gm7
C7
Dmaj7
G13♯11
F♯m7
Fm7
Em7
A7
Dmaj7
Gmaj7

F♯m7♭5
B7
Em7
Piano Solo
31
Bass Solo
32
Em7
F♯m7♭5
B7♭9
Em7
A7
D
Drums
3
Em7
A7
Dmaj7
Gmaj7
F♯m7
Fm7
Em7
Drums
3
Em7
F♯m7♭5
B7♭9
Em7
A7
Dmaj7
G13♯11
F♯m7
B7
Em7
Gm7
C7
Dmaj7
Gmaj7
F♯m7
Fdim7
Em7
A7
G♯m7♭5
G6/9
Dadd9/F♯
F13
Em7
A7♯9
Dmaj9

I Can't Get Started with You

Words by Ira Gershwin
Music by Vernon Duke

E♭ Alto Saxophone

C♯m7 F♯7 C♯m7 F♯7 C7♭9 Bmaj7 E7 Bmaj7
Bm Bm(maj7)/A♯ Bm7/A E7/G♯
C♯m7 F♯7♭9
Bm7 E7 Amaj7 F♯m7
Bm7 E7 G♯m7 C♯7 Gm7 C7
F♯m7 B7 Fm7 B♭7 Amaj7 F♯m7
Bm7 E7 Amaj7 F♯m7 Bm7 E7
Amaj7
Piano Solo
15
Bass Solo
15
C♯m7 F♯7
C♯m7 F♯7 Bmaj7 E7

Bmaj7
Bm
Bm(maj7)/A♯
Bm7/A
E7/G♯
C♯m7
C7
Fmaj7
B♭maj7
Amaj7
F♯m7
Bm7
E7
G♯m7
C♯7
Gm7
C7
F♯m7
B7
Fm7
B♭7
Amaj7
Dmaj7
C♯m7
F♯7
Bm7
E7♭9
Cadenza
N.C.
Amaj7

I Know That You Know

Words and Music by Vincent Youmans,
Otto Harbach and Anne Caldwell O'Dea

G7
Gm7
C7
F6/9
Rollins Solo
128
Trumpet Solo
95
Stitt Solo
G7
Gm7
C7
F6/9
Am7♭5
D7
G7
Gm7
G♭7
F6/9
Gm7
C7
F6/9
Am7
A♭m7
G7
Gm7
C7
Cm7
F7
B♭m7
E♭7
Am7
D7
G7

Gm7 C7 F6/9
G7 Gm7
C7 F6/9 Am7♭5
D7 G7 Gm7
C7 F6/9 Gm7 C7 F6/9
D7 G7 D♭m7
G♭7 Cm7 F7 B♭m7
E♭7 Am7 D7 G7
Gm7 C7 F6/9
3

G7
Gm7
C7
F6/9
Am7♭5
D7
G7
Gm7
C7
F6/9
Gm7
C7
F6/9
3
D7
G7
D♭m7
G♭7
Cm7
F7
B♭m7
E♭7
Am7
D7
G7
Gm7
C7
F6/9
Squeak
G7
Gm7

C7
F6/9
Am7♭5
D7
G7
D♭m7
G♭7
F6/9
Gm7
C7
F6/9
Am7♭5
D7
G7
Gm7
G♭7
Cm7
F7
B♭m7
E♭7
Am7
D7
G7
Gm7
C7
F6/9
G7
Trumpet
Tenor
Gm7
C7
F6/9
Am7♭5

D7 G7 Gm7
C7 F6/9 Am7
D7 G7 Gm7
C7 Cm7 F7 B♭m7
E♭7 Am7 D7 G7
Gm7 C7
D♭7 G♭maj7
Bmaj7 Emaj7
E♭maj7
Trumpet ad lib.

Moten Swing

By Buster Moten and Bennie Moten

G6 C7 Bm7 Em7 Am7 D7
A7 D7 G
C♯m7 F♯7 B6 G♯m7 C♯m7 F♯7
B6 G♯m7 C♯m7 F♯7 B6 G♯m7 C♯m7 F♯7 B6 E7
Am7 D7 G6 C7 Bm7 E Am7 D7
Bm7 E7 Am7 D7 G Em7 Am7 D7
G C7 Bm7 Em7 Am7 D7 Bm7 E7 A7
D7 G E7 Am7 D7 G C7
Bm7 Em7 Am7 D7 Bm7 E7 A7

D7 G6 C♯m7 F♯7
B6 G♯m7 C♯m7 F♯7 B6 G♯m7 C♯m7 F♯7
B6 G♯m7 C♯m7 F♯7 B6 E7 Am7 D7
G6 C7 Bm7 Em7 Am7 D7 Bm7 E7
A7 D7 G6 Em7 Am7 D7
G6 C7 Bm7 Em7 Am7 D7 Bm7♭5 E7 A7 D7
Bm7 B♭m7 Am7 D7 G6 C7
Bm7 E7 Am7 D7
Bm7 E7 A7 A♭7
G6 C♯m7 F♯7 B6 G♯m7

C♯m7 F♯7 B6 G♯m7 C♯m7 F♯7 B6 G♯m7
C♯m7 F♯7 B6 E7 Am7 D7 G C7
Bm7 Em7 Am7 D7 Bm7 E7 A7
Shake
D7 G Em7 Am7 D7
G
Piano Solo
62
G6 C7
Bm7 Em7 Am7 D7 Bm7 E7 A7
D7 G6 Em7 Am7 D7 G6 C7
Bm7 Em7 Am7 D7 Bm7♭5 E7 A7
D7 G6 C♯m7 F♯7 B6 G♯m7
C♯m7 F♯7 B6 G♯m7 C♯m7 F♯7
B6 G♯m7 C♯m7 F♯7 B6 E7 Am7 D7

G6 C7 Bm7 E7 Am7 D7 Bm7 E7 Am7
D7 G Em7 Am7 D7 G6 C7 Bm7 Em7 Am7 D7
Bm7 E7 A7 D7
Bm7 B♭m7 Am7 D7 G6 C7
Bm7 E7 Am7 D7 Bm7 E7
A7 D7 G
C♯m7 F♯7 B6 G♯m7 C♯m7 F♯7 B6 G♯m7 C♯m7 C7
B6 G♯m7 C♯m7 F♯7 B6 E7 Am7 D7
G6 C7 Bm7 E7 Am7 D7
A7 D7 G6

On the Sunny Side of the Street

Lyric by Dorothy Fields
Music by Jimmy McHugh

E♭maj7
D6/9
C♯m7
F♯7
Gmaj7
A7
F♯7/A♯
Bm7
3
E9♯11
3
Em7
A7
F♯m7
Fm7
3
Em7
A7
D6/9
3
C♯m7
F♯7
3
Gmaj7
A7
F♯7/A♯
Bm7
E9♯11
Em7
A7
D
D7
Gmaj7
E7
3
3
3
3
3
Em7
3
A7
3
3
D6/9
3
C♯m7
3
F♯7
Gmaj7
A7
F♯7/A♯
Bm7
E9♯11
Em7
A7
D
3

Trumpet Solo
31
Rollins Solo
32
Stitt Solo
D6/9
3
C♯m7
F♯7
Gmaj7
A7
F♯7/A♯
Bm7
E9♯11
Em7
A7
F♯m7
Fm7
Em7
A7
D6/9
Rollins Solo
C♯m7
F♯7
Gmaj7
A7
F♯7/A♯
Bm7
E9♯11
Em7
A7
D6/9
Stitt Solo
D7
Gmaj7
E7
A7
D6/9
C♯m7
F♯7
Gmaj7
A7
F♯7/A♯
Bm7
E9♯11
E7
E♭7
E7
E♭7
D
N.C.
E♭7
D6/9

Orange Ashtray

By Sonny Stitt

Fm7 B♭7 E♭7 C7 Fm7 B♭7
E♭7 A♭7 E♭7 B♭m7 E♭7
A♭7 E♭7 Gm7 C7
Fm7 B♭7 E♭7 C7 Fm7 B♭7
E♭7 A♭7 E♭7 B♭m7 E♭7
A♭7 E♭7 Gm7 C7
Fm7 B♭7 E♭7 C7 Fm7 B♭7
E♭7 A♭7 E♭7 B♭m7 E♭7
A♭7 E♭7 Gm7 C7

Fm7 B♭7 E♭7 C7 Fm7 B♭7
E♭7 A♭7 E♭7 B♭m7 E♭7
A♭7 E♭7 F♯m7 B7
Fm7 B♭7 E♭7 C7 Fm7 B♭7
E♭7 A♭7 E♭7 B♭m7 E♭7
A♭7 E♭7 Gm7 C7
Fm7 B♭7 E♭7 C7 Fm7 B♭7
E♭7 A♭7 E♭7 B♭m7 E♭7
A♭7 E♭7 Gm7 C7

Fm7 B♭7 E♭7 C7 Fm7 B♭7
E♭7 A♭7 E♭7 B♭m7 E♭7
A♭7 E♭7 Gm7 C7
Fm7 B♭7 Gm7 C7
Fm7 B♭7 Gm7 C7
Fm7 B♭7 Gm7 C7
Fm7 B♭7 Gm7 C7
Fm7 B♭7 Gm7 C7
Fm7 B♭7 Gm7 C7

Fm7 B♭7 Gm7 C7
Fm7 B♭7 Gm7 C7
Fm7 B♭7 Gm7 C7
Fm7 B♭7 Gm7
C7 Fm7 B♭7 Gm7
C7 Fm7 B♭7 E♭
Fm7 B♭7 E♭
Fm7 B♭7 E♭
Fm7 B♭7 E♭

Ray's Idea

By Walter Gil Fuller and Raymond Brown

Cm7 F7♯5 Dm7 G7♭9 Cm7 F7
B♭7 E♭maj7 E♭m7 A♭7 Cm7 F7 B♭6/9
Fm7 B♭7 E♭m7
A♭7 D♭m7 G♭7 Cm7
F7 B♭6/9 Gm7 Cm7 F7♯5 Dm7 G7♭9
Cm7 F7 B♭7 E♭maj7 E♭m7 A♭7
Cm7 F7♯5 B♭6/9 F7 B♭6/9 Gm7 Cm7 F7♯5
Dm7 G7♭9 Cm7 F7 B♭7 E♭maj7 E♭m7 A♭7
Dm7 G7♭9 Cm7 F7 B♭6/9 Gm7 Cm7 F7♯5

Dm7 G7♭9 Cm7 F7 B♭7
E♭maj7 E♭m7 A♭7 Cm7 F7 B♭6/9 Fm7
B♭7 E♭m7 A♭7 D♭m7 G♭7
Cm7 F7 B♭6/9 Gm7 Cm7 F7♯5
Dm7 D♭m7 Cm7 F7 B♭7
E♭maj7 E♭m7 A♭7 Cm7 F7♯5 B♭ F7 B♭6/9
Piano Solo
30
B♭6/9 Gm7 Cm7 F7♯5 Dm7 G7♭9 Cm7 F7
B♭7 E♭maj7 E♭m7 A♭ Dm7 G7♭9 Cm7 F7

Bb6/9 Gm7 Cm7 F7#5 Dm7 G7b9
Cm7 F7 Bb7 Ebmaj7 Ebm7 Ab7
3
Cm7 F7 Bb6/9 Fm7 Bb7
Ebm7 Ab7 Dbm7 Gb7
Cm7 3 Gbm7 B7 Bb6/9 Gm7
Cm7 F7#5 Dm7 G7 Cm7 3 B7#9
Bb7 3 Eb Ebm7 Ab7 Cm7 F7
Bb6/9 Gm7 Cm7 F7b9 Bb

Soul Shack

By Sonny Stitt

Dm7 G7 C7 A7 Dm7 G7
C7
F7 C7 Em7 A7
Dm7 G7 C7
F7 C7
F7 C7 Em7♭5 A7
Dm7 G7 C7
F7 C7 Em7♭5 A7
Dm7 G7 C7

F7
C7
Em7
A7
Dm7
G7
C7
F7
C7
Em7
E♭m7
Dm7
G7
C7
A7
Dm7
G7
C7
F7
C7
Em7
A7
Dm7
G7
C7

F7 C7 Em7♭5 A7
D7 G7 C7 A7 Dm7 G7
C7
F7 C7 Em7♭5 A7
Dm7 G7 C7
F7 C7 Em7♭5 A7
Dm7 G7 C7
Organ Solo
80
C7

F7 C7 A7
Dm7 G7 C7
F7 C7
F7 C7 Em7♭5 A7
Dm7 G7 C7
F7 C7 A7
Dm7 G7 C7
F7 C7 A7

Dm7
G7
C7
F7
C7
A7
Dm7
G7
C7
F7
C7
Em7
A7
Dm7
G7
C7
F7
C7
E♭m7
Dm7
G7
C7

F7 C7 Em7 A7
Dm7 G7 C7 A7 Dm7 G7
C7
F7 C7 Em7 A7
Dm7 G7 C7
F F♯dim7 C A7
D7 G7 Em7 A7 Dm7 E♭dim7
Em7 A7 Dm7 G7 Em7
A7 Dm7 G7 C7

Tune Up

By Miles Davis

B♭ Tenor Saxophone

Stitt Solo

F♯m7
B7
Emaj7
Em7
A7
Dmaj7
Dm7
G7
Cmaj7
F♯m7
G7
Cmaj7
F7
F♯m7
B7
Emaj7
Em7
A7
Dmaj7
Dm7
G7
Cmaj7
F♯m7
G7
Cmaj7
F7
F♯m7
B7
Emaj7
Em7
A7
Dmaj7

Dm7 G7 Cmaj7
F♯m7 G7 Cmaj7 F7
F♯m7 B7 Emaj7
Em7 A7 Dmaj7
Dm7 G7 Cmaj7
F♯m7 G7 Cmaj7 F7
F♯m7 B7 Emaj7
Em7 A7 Dmaj7
Dm7 G7 Cmaj7
F♯m7 G7 Cmaj7 F7
3

F♯m7
B7
Emaj7
Em7
A7
Dmaj7
Dm7
G7
Cmaj7
F♯m7
G7
Cmaj7
F7
F♯m7
B7
Emaj7
Em7
A7
Dmaj7
Dm7
G7
Cmaj7
F♯m7
G7
Cmaj7
F7
F♯m7
B7
Emaj7
Em7
A7
Dmaj7

Dm7 G7 Cmaj7
F♯m7 G7 Cmaj7 F7
F♯m7 B7 Emaj7
Em7 A7 Dmaj7
Dm7 G7 Cmaj7
F♯m7 G7 Cmaj7 F7
F♯m7 B7 Emaj7
Em7 A7 Dmaj7
Dm7 G7 Cmaj7
F♯m7 G7 Cmaj7 F7

F♯m7
B7
Emaj7
Em7
A7
Dmaj7
Dm7
G7
Cmaj7
F♯m7
G7
Cmaj7
F7
F♯m7
B7
Piano Solo
74
F♯m7
G7
Cmaj7
F7
F♯m7
B7
Emaj7
Em7
A7
Dmaj7
Dm7
G7
Cmaj7
F♯m7
G7

Cmaj7 F7 F♯m7 B7
Emaj7 Em7 A7
Dmaj7 Dm7 G7
Cmaj7 F♯m7 G7
Cmaj7 F7 F♯m7 B7
Emaj7 Em7 A7
Dmaj7 Dm7 G7
Cmaj7 F♯m7 G7
Cmaj7 F7 F♯m7 B7
3 3

Emaj7
Em7
A7
Dmaj7
Dm7
G7
Cmaj7
F♯m7
G7
Cmaj7
F7
F♯m7
G7
Cmaj7
F7
F♯m7
G7
Cmaj7
F7
Emaj7
3

ARTIST TRANSCRIPTIONS®

Artist Transcriptions are authentic, note-for-note transcriptions of today's hottest artists in jazz, pop and rock. These outstanding, accurate arrangements are in an easy-to-read format which includes all essential lines. Artist Transcriptions can be used to perform, sequence or for reference.

CLARINET

00672423	Buddy De Franco Collection	$19.95

FLUTE

00672379	Eric Dolphy Collection	$19.95
00672372	James Moody Collection – Sax and Flute	$19.95
00660108	James Newton – Improvising Flute	$14.95
00672455	Lew Tabackin Collection	$19.95

GUITAR & BASS

00660113	The Guitar Style of George Benson	$14.95
00672331	Ron Carter – Acoustic Bass	$16.95
00660115	Al Di Meola – Friday Night in San Francisco	$14.95
00604043	Al Di Meola – Music, Words, Pictures	$14.95
00673245	Jazz Style of Tal Farlow	$19.95
00672359	Bela Fleck and the Flecktones	$18.95
00699389	Jim Hall – Jazz Guitar Environments	$19.95
00699306	Jim Hall – Exploring Jazz Guitar	$19.95
00672335	Best of Scott Henderson	$24.95
00672356	Jazz Guitar Standards	$19.95
00675536	Wes Montgomery – Guitar Transcriptions	$17.95
00672353	Joe Pass Collection	$18.95
00673216	John Patitucci	$16.95
00672374	Johnny Smith Guitar Solos	$16.95
00672320	Mark Whitfield	$19.95
00672337	Gary Willis Collection	$19.95

PIANO & KEYBOARD

00672338	Monty Alexander Collection	$19.95
00672487	Monty Alexander Plays Standards	$19.95
00672318	Kenny Barron Collection	$22.95
00672520	Count Basie Collection	$19.95
00672364	Warren Bernhardt Collection	$19.95
00672439	Cyrus Chestnut Collection	$19.95
00673242	Billy Childs Collection	$19.95
00672300	Chick Corea – Paint the World	$12.95
00672537	Bill Evans at Town Hall	$16.95
00672425	Bill Evans – Piano Interpretations	$19.95
00672365	Bill Evans – Piano Standards	$19.95
00672510	Bill Evans Trio – Vol. 1: 1959-1961	$24.95
00672511	Bill Evans Trio – Vol. 2: 1962-1965	$24.95
00672512	Bill Evans Trio – Vol. 3: 1968-1974	$24.95
00672513	Bill Evans Trio – Vol. 4: 1979-1980	$24.95
00672329	Benny Green Collection	$19.95
00672486	Vince Guaraldi Collection	$19.95
00672419	Herbie Hancock Collection	$19.95
00672446	Gene Harris Collection	$19.95
00672438	Hampton Hawes	$19.95
00672322	Ahmad Jamal Collection	$22.95
00672476	Brad Mehldau Collection	$19.95
00672390	Thelonious Monk Plays Jazz Standards – Volume 1	$19.95
00672391	Thelonious Monk Plays Jazz Standards – Volume 2	$19.95
00672433	Jelly Roll Morton – The Piano Rolls	$12.95
00672542	Oscar Peterson – Jazz Piano Solos	$14.95
00672544	Oscar Peterson – Originals	$9.95
00672532	Oscar Peterson – Plays Broadway	$19.95
00672531	Oscar Peterson – Plays Duke Ellington	$19.95
00672533	Oscar Peterson – Trios	$24.95
00672543	Oscar Peterson Trio – Canadiana Suite	$7.95
00672534	Very Best of Oscar Peterson	$22.95
00672371	Bud Powell Classics	$19.95
00672376	Bud Powell Collection	$19.95
00672437	André Previn Collection	$19.95
00672507	Gonzalo Rubalcaba Collection	$19.95
00672303	Horace Silver Collection	$19.95
00672316	Art Tatum Collection	$22.95
00672355	Art Tatum Solo Book	$19.95
00672357	Billy Taylor Collection	$24.95
00673215	McCoy Tyner	$16.95
00672321	Cedar Walton Collection	$19.95
00672519	Kenny Werner Collection	$19.95
00672434	Teddy Wilson Collection	$19.95

SAXOPHONE

00673244	Julian "Cannonball" Adderley Collection	$19.95
00673237	Michael Brecker	$19.95
00672429	Michael Brecker Collection	$19.95
00672351	Brecker Brothers... And All Their Jazz	$19.95
00672447	Best of the Brecker Brothers	$19.95
00672315	Benny Carter Plays Standards	$22.95
00672314	Benny Carter Collection	$22.95
00672394	James Carter Collection	$19.95
00672349	John Coltrane Plays Giant Steps	$19.95
00672529	John Coltrane – Giant Steps	$14.95
00672494	John Coltrane – A Love Supreme	$14.95
00672493	John Coltrane Plays "Coltrane Changes"	$19.95
00672453	John Coltrane Plays Standards	$19.95
00673233	John Coltrane Solos	$22.95
00672328	Paul Desmond Collection	$19.95
00672454	Paul Desmond – Standard Time	$19.95
00672379	Eric Dolphy Collection	$19.95
00672530	Kenny Garrett Collection	$19.95
00699375	Stan Getz	$18.95
00672377	Stan Getz – Bossa Novas	$19.95
00672375	Stan Getz – Standards	$17.95
00673254	Great Tenor Sax Solos	$18.95
00672523	Coleman Hawkins Collection	$19.95
00673252	Joe Henderson – Selections from "Lush Life" & "So Near So Far"	$19.95
00672330	Best of Joe Henderson	$22.95
00673239	Best of Kenny G	$19.95
00673229	Kenny G – Breathless	$19.95
00672462	Kenny G – Classics in the Key of G	$19.95
00672485	Kenny G – Faith: A Holiday Album	$14.95
00672373	Kenny G – The Moment	$19.95
00672516	Kenny G – Paradise	$14.95
00672326	Joe Lovano Collection	$19.95
00672498	Jackie McLean Collection	$19.95
00672372	James Moody Collection – Sax and Flute	$19.95
00672416	Frank Morgan Collection	$19.95
00672539	Gerry Mulligan Collection	$19.95
00672352	Charlie Parker Collection	$19.95
00672444	Sonny Rollins Collection	$19.95
00675000	David Sanborn Collection	$16.95
00672528	Bud Shank Collection	$19.95
00672491	New Best of Wayne Shorter	$19.95
00672455	Lew Tabackin Collection	$19.95
00672334	Stanley Turrentine Collection	$19.95
00672524	Lester Young Collection	$19.95

TROMBONE

00672332	J.J. Johnson Collection	$19.95
00672489	Steve Turré Collection	$19.95

TRUMPET

00672480	Louis Armstrong Collection	$14.95
00672481	Louis Armstrong Plays Standards	$14.95
00672435	Chet Baker Collection	$19.95
00673234	Randy Brecker	$17.95
00672351	Brecker Brothers... And All Their Jazz	$19.95
00672447	Best of the Brecker Brothers	$19.95
00672448	Miles Davis – Originals, Vol. 1	$19.95
00672451	Miles Davis – Originals, Vol. 2	$19.95
00672450	Miles Davis – Standards, Vol. 1	$19.95
00672449	Miles Davis – Standards, Vol. 2	$19.95
00672479	Dizzy Gillespie Collection	$19.95
00673214	Freddie Hubbard	$14.95
00672382	Tom Harrell – Jazz Trumpet	$19.95
00672363	Jazz Trumpet Solos	$9.95
00672506	Chuck Mangione Collection	$19.95
00672525	Arturo Sandoval – Trumpet Evolution	$19.95

FOR MORE INFORMATION, SEE YOUR LOCAL MUSIC DEALER, OR WRITE TO:

HAL•LEONARD® CORPORATION
7777 W. BLUEMOUND RD. P.O. BOX 13819 MILWAUKEE, WI 53213

Visit our web site for a complete listing of our titles with songlists at www.halleonard.com

Prices and availability subject to change without notice.